This Orchard
book belongs to

_____

_____

_____

For George, Katriona, Luke, Rachel and Christian – G.S.
Pour Marie-Julia – S.B.

ORCHARD BOOKS
338 Euston Road, London NW1 3BH
Orchard Books Australia
Level 17/207 Kent Street, Sydney, NSW 2000

First published in 2008 by Orchard Books
First published in paperback in 2009

ISBN 978 1 84362 546 9

Text © Gillian Shields 2008
Illustrations © Sebastien Braun 2008

The rights of Gillian Shields to be identified as the author
and of Sebastien Braun to be identified as the illustrator
of this book have been asserted by them in accordance
with the Copyright, Designs and Patents Act, 1988.

A CIP catalogue record for this book is available from the British Library.

1 3 5 7 9 10 8 6 4 2

Printed in Malaysia

Orchard Books is a division of Hachette Children's Books, an Hachette Livre UK company.
www.hachettelivre.co.uk

The Beginner's Guide to
Teddy Bears

Gillian Shields   Sebastien Braun

ORCHARD BOOKS

You need a bear
And a bear needs you.

You and a bear
Together make two.

What do you look for in a bear?

Soft, gentle, cuddly and warm.

Big. . .

or small!

Bears like games
In the shining sun,
Though wind and rain
And snow can be fun.

W
hat kind of weather do bears like best?

Sunny days,

rainy days,

snowy days

and windy days.

All kinds
of weather!

Bears love playing,
Bears love toys,
Bears love making
Lots of NOISE!

What toys do bears like best?

Dressing-up clothes . . .

bouncy balls, ducks to push . . .

and pedal cars.
Vroom! Vroom!

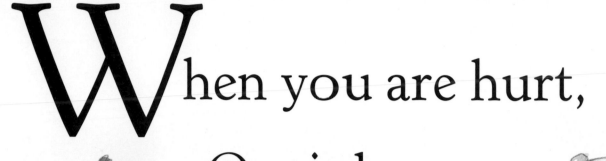

When you are hurt,

Or sick,

or sad,

Only your bear

Can make you glad.

What do bears need when they don't feel well?

A cuddly pillow . . .

lemonade in bed, a doctor's kit.

Bears love eating
Everything yummy.
Picnics are best for
A bear's hungry tummy.

What do bears love to eat?

Honey, jellybeans, lollipops . . .

ice cream and honey (again).

When it is late
And time for bed,
You cannot sleep
Without your ted.

What do bears need at bedtime?

A cuddly toy and a special blanket.

A glass of milk, night-lights,
a toothbrush and a bedtime story.

Every bear loves
A big bear hug,
Soft and cosy,
Warm and snug.

W ho needs a bear?

You need a bear
And a bear needs you.

You and a bear
Together make two.